THE

JOURNEYS

OF A

FRAGILE

HEART

MAJVOR SABINE AKSOY

American Literary Press, Inc.
Five Star Special Edition
Baltimore, Maryland

THE JOURNEYS OF A FRAGILE HEART

Library of Congress
Cataloging in Publication Data
ISBN 1-56167-615-2

Library of Congress Card Catalog Number:
00-190048

First Edition

Published by

American Literary Press, Inc.
Five Star Special Edition
8019 Belair Road, Suite 10
Baltimore, Maryland 21236

Manufactured in the United States of America

THE THANKING NOTE

Special thanks to my mother: Naile Aksoy
for supporting me and guiding me through life. You are my HERO!
My sisters: Leila Balaci, Christina Balaci and Renate Ursula Aksoy
for believing in my writing.
Special thanks to Andreas Balaci for the use of his computer,
Jason Balaci, John Balaci and Yakup Balaci.
My dad: May God bless your soul in rest and peace—
Aziz Aksoy (1937-1983).
Collen Williams and Diane Lowe for guiding me through the
English language.
D. Grant Isaac, Margaret Mcarthy,
Rene Arnolis, Paul Fogg; (That's Nice!)
Trudy Pack, Jaki Yepremian, Melina Neyra, Isabella Pyziak,
Donna Kaczmarcyk, Lya Hernandez,
Douglas Williamth Hogarth, Greg Cyfko,
Phil Elder, Barry McKinnon, Stephen Worrall
for all their faith, support, and inspiration.

For everyone else:
I DID IT!

Special Thanks to all the staff members of
American Literary Press

THE JOURNEY OF A FRAGILE HEART

IN A SMALL VILLAGE CALLED TUMBA IN STOCKHOLM, SWEDEN,
A CHILD IS BORN; FOR A MOMENT HAPPINESS SURROUNDS THE
FAMILY, SOON LIFE CHANGED,
WHEN THE MOTHER GETS IN A CAR ACCIDENT AND BECOMES
CRITICALLY INJURED FOR SEVERAL YEARS.
DURING ALL THIS; FATHER PASSED AWAY FROM CANCER LEAVING
BEHIND FOUR YOUNG DAUGHTERS AND A WIFE WHO NEEDED HIM
THE MOST.

FOR EVERY LAUGHTER AND JOY THAT A NEW BORN BROUGHT AND
HAD BROUGHT; TRAGEDY TOOK OVER AND SHATTERED TEARS OF
PAIN, LOSS, AND BETRAYAL TO A FAMILY SO PERFECT.

THE STRENGTH OF A MOTHER WHO NEVER GAVE UP ALL OF FAITH,
LOVE, DISCIPLINE AND CARE; HEALED ALL OF WOUNDED SCARS
WHETHER PHYSICAL OR EMOTIONAL.
BUT NO MATTER HOW HEALED, SOME THINGS ARE NEVER
FORGOTTEN AND CAN NEVER BE LEFT BEHIND.

THROUGH GOOD TIMES AND BAD, A CHILD GREW UP,
ME!, HEART BROKEN SINCE BIRTH, OPENED HER FIRST EYES WITH
A FATHER, BUT ALL REMEMBRANCE WITHOUT.
THE HEART BROKEN IN HALF, ONE HALF TAKEN AWAY WHILE THE
OTHER STILL BEATS FROM THE LOVE OF A MOTHER AND SISTERS.

BECAUSE OF ALL THIS!
ANOTHER POET CREATED,
MAJVOR SABINE AKSOY
THROUGH ALL EXPERIENCES,
TURNED TO POETRY AS A WAY OF LETTING PERSONAL FEELINGS,
EMOTIONS AND DREAMS OUT IN WORDS.

DAY IN AND DAY OUT, I THINK ABOUT ALL THE THINGS THAT MY
MEMORIES ARE MADE OF AND I GET ALTERNATELY FASCINATED
AND REPULSED BY THE VARIETY OF LIFE—ALL ITS SOUNDS,
COLOURS, MOVEMENTS AND SHAPES, THAT IS WHEN I BECOME
CAPABLE OF PRODUCING SOMETHING VERY TRUE AND HEARTFELT.

I WRITE OF TIME, EMOTIONS EXPERIENCED IN LIFE,
FEELINGS THAT BECOME PART OF OUR HEARTBEAT AND OTHERS
HOW I DREAM THEM TO BE;
ALL ARE A COMBINATION OF MY INWARD AND OUTWARD
INFLUENCES.

FOR EVERY WORD THAT IS PLACED IN CONTACT WITH ANOTHER
ARE WORDS OF TRUE EXPERIENCES, ALL DEDICATED TO A
SPECIAL SOMEONE OR SOMETHING THAT HAD AN EFFECT IN MY
HEARTBEAT.

ALL OF LOVE,

MAJVOR SABINE AKSOY

Contents

CHILDHOOD

Like the weather I live
not knowing if it will rain, snow or get sunshine
like the falling rain I cry
like the snow I melt
like the sunshine I am capable of love.

In a world so alone
only reflections lived
when life ages and takes childhood away
in bits and pieces where I felt no pain
but living happiness.

Like a seed I grew older,
fresh and new
childhood forced away
when challenge steps ahead.

Heart of a child so broken
when taken for granted
regardless of what I feel,
like or want,
childhood is over.

Dolls are packed away
I walk away from fantasy into reality
where the sky is dark and cold
my body still and chilled
when I scream out at night
nobody is willing to listen
because I am no longer a child.

I try talking to myself
but in me there are no answers

where I stand
I soon drift off…

When I awake
the sun glittered above and gave me warmth.

A sudden hero appeared with a key
that is when I soon accepted now as is
over childhood that was.

PEACEFUL

I moved on with my lonely cry…
through my tears I see river,
flowers and the trees
all sitting outside softly in the breeze
I wish I could be so peaceful.

I see leaves being blown to a place
where I never knew existed,
a reflection of someone's face lies among
the leafs reflecting on my heart so gentle.

Soon I found comfort
just like nature
I knew I reached a place
that never existed,
a place so peaceful
I do not want to wake up.

DREAM OF LOVE

In a world so true,
in a heart so whole,
through a dream wished upon...
Deep inside I believed truth
but in reality truth never lived.
My heart you broke like glass
my happiness you turn to pain...
when I open my eyes
I realized this was a dream of love.

BURNING

Heard screaming at night
I can hear myself
someone is talking
I can not hear myself
the wind whispers my name,
there is nobody there.

Shadows walking towards the stars,
I run late
I do not know where to go
I do not know what to say
it is not easy to put out for what
is loving.

Lost between roads of life
torn between happiness and pain
running without action
feelings without love.

As I break down to cry
heaven opens up

guides me from last to first
as all the other see
and die of thirst.

PACIFIC DREAM

Brightness wakes me up in the morning
everything is silent and cold
shadowed words of feelings with no movement,
no motion; it is all quiet.
Walking towards the blue river,
I can sense the soft mellow breeze,
I can feel the warmth from the glowing sun
as I see the fresh scented palms
close when I start to cry.

The river flow, turns and bends,
a whisper from the wind,
music to my ears.
The sky glittering like million diamonds
on a sea and I feel an unknown peace.

The river started running deeper
than it ever ran before…
soon I found colours above shine bright
through the eyes of love;
when the misty shadows appear
the never ending beauty I hear.

Some voice deep inside calls my name
through all the beauty in misty skies,
you walked the road of destiny and
the road lead you to me,
now we stand together but so far away.

Reach for my hand,
let's become safe and sound
with shadowed words
with nature's truth meant to be,
where there will be no doubt
when you are with me.

Together we have changed the river and the sky
now the scented palms that open when we walk by,
exploring as they grow to open the doors of life
and the sand forms the tree magic words of love.
Only the whisper from the wind moves us together tightly,
in this Island of love where I wake up from a Pacific Dream.

DOWN THE WINDOW CORNER

Looking down the upstairs window
all I see is clear
where life shines through so crystal clear.

I see people,
so full of joy and laughter
while others are in pain;
…wonder what is to blame.

Beside a stairway,
I see my dream
just down the upstairs window
yet million miles away
full of laughter with evil.

As I freeze beside the window corner
I recall the first sight
the look so true
the face so soft like the delicate of a baby

I can feel it as it fades away
from my distance.

When I soon realize myself stearring
at a glass full of ice
where I froze of dying love.

PURE DOVE

All this time
dreaming of a place I may never visit
a place where hearts are one
a place where lonelyness does not exist.

Soon a dove come flying by my distance
made me realize what life is all about
that is when my soul learned to live.

All again
two lives with two different livings
one not compared to mine
one where freedom to fly
where my own
I may never walk.

In a life where loneliness does not exist
when my own is still living,
I crossed my heart and left
and now the pure dove is gone
and I must let it go because I could
not live the same.

WITH A GOOD-BYE

It is too late to say how I feel
it is too late to hope
it is too late for a hug or a kiss
and a way too late to say..
"it is you I miss"
what you have done
I may never forget
but one day you'll be sorry
and my heart, yours will regret.

In so many ways you were oh, so wrong
you wished to play it rough
and you have got it your way
you thought feelings were made of steel
but mine can never be so strong
but one day I will prove you wrong.

From a perfect start
you waste it all
why leave when you promised
you'll stay
why show care
when you threw it away
why forget
the most important day
why not use the words that
we wish to say
why do I laugh
when I really want to cry?
Why must we forget the heart with a good-bye?

REVEALED FEELINGS

Knowing these will be the last few words
I shall ever share with you again
I expect nothing more from you.

If there was ever a part of you that cared
sincerely,
I ask only that you cherish what is said in these few lines,
for I shall finally reveal to you all of me
that you have never known.

All things in life have a beginning and an end….. that so
follows
our beginning was one that come unexpectedly but highly
welcomed
I realized that I had a friend
that very first time,
you sat next to me
we said little that day,
I was in cure of you.
Being younger
we were the best of friends
we'd much later become.

If only you could have known how much I admired you,
not one single moment would go by before
I'd look for that instant turn of mind
to thoughts of you.
You might have felt that your innocence was a hidden
that you have so often tried to part with
but it was a quality I had fallen in love with immediately.

LIVE IT CLEAR

Just like the air in heaven I breathe
like a bird flying through the sky
I follow footsteps
when shadows quide me toward an empty air
without touch, I feel you
without a picture, I see you
I'll betray life and death to hear you.

I am living a dream
so hopeless
when I betray the truth of it all.

Between closed doors
your shadow leaves me
without bothering you want to see me
life becomes so blurry day after day
yet we live it as it is so clear.

NO LONGER

What do I gain by losing you?
What do I have left without you?
Is this true love?
I thought true love was complete?
But now you have taken your piece of it all
and the heat is no longer a whole.

TO FAIL IS ANOTHER MEANING OF LIFE

In life we must take chances,
most often we fail
but that is the only way we will
be able to grow as we learn to know

the meaning of life.

Never give up on a dream that seems
out of reach;
we dream for a reason.

If you reach that dream and fail…
just remember you have not failed
but gained an experience
and another meaning of life.

I NO LONGER NEED YOU

You showd me sadness when I needed
care,
you brought me a casket when I needed
life,
you started to scream when I needed
you to sing,
NOW
you bring me your care when I need it
least,
you bring me your company when I need
you to leave,
you start to sing when I need to
scream.

HIS REFLECTIONS

Lost in jumbled dreams,
a young man discovering
everything is not what it seems,
his emotions sweep in and out
like a confusing tide,
drawing me into his strange and
turbulent ride.

He wanders through another's web of lies,
my soul descends and flies,
I can see that reality is just beyond his hold,
the deception is not what he has been told.

Clings to an anchor in this sea of sad blue,
he finds out that now his refuge has vanished too,
all he loves has traveled far away,
only shattered dreams and confusion has stayd.

Many are the storms I've been through;
this time he is learning the hard way,
all he hopes are not be true,
but still he tries reflecting and wondering
what he can do.

SECOND PLACE

No one meets his sadness,
no one hears his cries,
he feels like the forsaken one
living all alone without her.

Crawls to desolate corners
fearing the unknown,
afraid to show himself,
he is hiding true feelings,
stashing them on shelves
where chosen ones run life's race,
wanting to be winners
while he knows he is settling
for second place.

ROAD OF LOVE

Love is a road we will one day take
when you least expect to go there,
your heart will drive you there
whether you want it to or not.

There your heart will swell
and tie it up like a knot,
you won't know what it is or
how you ever ended up there.

But you will feel it inside,
your feelings for another's heart
will well up inside.

Then no matter how far,
and no matter how near..
each road with a word or phrase
that created a whole heart
will always hold dear.

FOR YOU

When I walk into that store your heart once wore
I hear a voice and turn around,
praying it would be you I find,
but it is not you
and I am let down
and I keep walking with a frown.

A frown I've had for a year
it won't leave me
til your heart wakes you up from
your sleep.

I know you'll realize me again one day,
but when you do,
everything won't be the same,
I won't be able to remember the good times we shared,
or all those days when you laughed
and brightened my day.

I could still hear your sweet voice
deep inside,
it is in my mind,
I close my eyes and remember your smile
that once shared my own
and that shining face that still remain in my mind
to make my life worthwhile.

At this point,
my poem I'll conclude
I must say; if you ever knew how much
I cared that you have avoided
you would never have the courage
to speak to me again.

NOW YOU KNOW

You did not think I was very special
deep inside,
when I've got feelings and I've got pride,
you did not realize that
what I have to offer is more than
what you can give....

Until...
you gave up on my looks and
took a look beneath the surface of my skin,
and found me deep within;

with mind, heart and a true soul
that turned someone like you with a
one track mind depend on me
who at one time meant
nothing to you

After all that hurt caused,
now it all comes back,
but time which
subdues the memories and eases
away my pain,
here you stand alone;
vulnerable for her,
who only brings you rain.

FUTURE OF A PAST

In life, roads come and roads go
all the time wasted never comes back,
the words said can never be forgotten,
feelings that are broken can never heal
even when forgiven.

When times are rough
the heart forgets its true meaning,
it loses its sensitivity to evil
and becomes another heart.

When the temporary suffering is over,
you try to turn back time
but there is no such thing as turning back time,
the past can not be used to create a future.

The words said of evil
in time of pain,

remain til the end of time,
sometimes happiness is torn in pieces
and nothing can mend them
back together

WORTH

Dream dreams worth dreaming
hope hopes worth waiting for
and nature will take care of the future.

CONFUSION

My words do not speak how much I want to stay,
but force may never reveal how much I need to go,
the heart can never travel through such confusion
the way it is traveling.

Do I choose present happiness over the futures?
Or should I betray a better future over happiness I now
have?

But...

What is the knowledge without a tomorrow?
How will better jewels ease all of sorrow?
Must I later choose to borrow?

Then again...

What is today's happiness hold my place in a future?
Where would I be when they all leave?
Would I be able to lose this chance that life only brings
when least expected to?,
just because this time happiness I choose not to leave.

The winds give trouble to the mind,
making the night so long and cold
where confusion brings tears,
when morning brings light;
nature's melody direct me nowhere,
where I am lonely and scared
and unable to handle decisions.

Open my heart...
take a look deep inside of it all,
understand its beat
feel its softness
and listen to its words,
maybe you can recreate my roads.

THE JEMMIES

Like a garden full of nature's different colours,
where happiness grows in different forms
making beauty even more beautiful,
turning a simple smile into so much laughter
simply by words that touch the heart
and of actions made of care.

It is a place understanding and sensitivity exists
where differences are same
and similarities are one.

When I think of this place
I know happiness exists.
When I dream of this place
I awake with joy and so much laughter,
when I look back
so many memories bring me strength
because I am always with the jemmies

ACTION WITH NO THOUGHT!

Which direction did I look?
Where did I go?
When I needed a new hello.

Which road did I choose?
What did my heart believe?
When I did not need to leave.

Which is good and bad?
What am I supposed to do
when all I become,
I now blew?.....

HEART

I know it might hurt
I know we sorrow the most
I know we think that we have all
faith necessary to move mountains,
but when something involves the heart;
we are all losers because we become weak.

We must believe that everything comes and goes
for a good reason,
because if the heart did not accept
It sure was not meant to be.

SHARE ME

When you come…
come with lots of dreams
bring me your strength,

17

set me like a seal on your heart
hold my hand, let us become one,
bring me love
strong as death
suprise me like a flash,
give me warmth like the
warmth of fire,
bring the flame that is the touch of you.

DID I LIE TO MYSELF?

When thought the definition of friendship
completed the meaning of the heart,
lied to myself;
just as much I experienced lies.

Then comes the heart,
taken for granted…
needed for a friend when mostly missed,
but blinded by it when given.

Showing a friend kindness
as a honour of true friendship
but appreciated with no respect.

You come to me when you're in need of me
I am a friend when no one else wants to be
I am special when everyone else has left
I am a stranger not a friend when you're my friend.

No more…
our friendship has shown its true side
ignorance and lies has taken over the heart
I am no longer lies to myself
but I am a lier to what you have shown to be.

I do not need a friend
I do not need a partner
I do not need kindness that lasts for seconds
I do not need your betrayal that lasts a lifetime.

All I need is my heart to stay whole.

NEVER HARD

Do not tell me that love is hard...someone once said:
"there is no difficulty that enough feelings will not
conquer...
and there is no door that enough trust will not open,
there is no wood that enough care will not bridge,
there is no sin that enough understanding will not redeem
there is no wall that enough of true love will not throw
down,"
so before you throw your dreams away
find the inner strength in you
and there will be nothing hard in life.

CAPABLE

Why do you not love all persons?
Do not tell me you are not capable of love!
If you truly love one person,
you love all persons
you love the world that brought you this person,
you love life because life brought you here.

If you are able to say "I love you" and mean it
then you must be capable of love for all
and yourself.

HOW DOES IT WORK

There is difficulty involved when in love,
the fear of falling in love with a character not a
personality
but do not fear because to love does not consist in gazing
at each other
but in taking a look together in the same direction.

ANOTHER FALL HAS COME

Cold breeze…
the wind blowing leaves place to place,
sunshine has left its warmth,
footprints of a past distanced away;

hear the cry of a young woman
the strength within a broken heart…
hears the memories
wishes for a new life.

Words of promises
now haunt for my leave
touch of eternity
now betrayed true believe
laughter of joy
now proven to be
the smile of a boy.

Through a mirror…at fall
life reflects
the world a funny place
the humans toys to the soul.
see us
closer then further away

happy less than cry
friends but more like enemies.

REMAIN MY ETERNITY

Across the room...crowded
numb by the sight of you
touched by the untouchable
heard by the unspoken
understood from a different language.

We see colours
using sight starring at the same
living soul
nature sends messages to the heart
from a look so innocent
yet hidden from the world.

If the heart caught the magic feeling
this will remain eternity.

FORGIVE BUT CAN'T FORGET

Knowing failure is an experience
never a loss,
the mind loosens up its aches of pain
and belives in just another falling rain.

The mind; a mind of its own
the heart; the beat of fullfillment,
when broken nothing is kept as a token,

what will always remain are the memories
that time can never take away,
tears that do not wash away,

pain will never betray
all that has happened
because the scars will always stay.

....through the mind we
are able to forgive
but through the heart we are unable to forget.

GIFTED BY HEAVEN

Did heaven guide me here?
Was the soul of a father gifted to another?
When you choose him among all other.

Are you watching over me through another's eyes?
Are you speaking to me through another's speech?
Are you listening to me through another's heart?
Because he's been like a father from the start.

HOW MUCH GOOD AND BAD

After all this time,
I look back through all the good and bad,
among the good of then
I find the bad in now,
through the bad in now
I find the good in then
...yet either way happiness never existed.

When the soul is taken for granted
by the sweet lies of a wolf,
all of promises are left undone
by the heart that never really had a beat
because this happiness never found its seat.

So where may I end an
ended beginning
when after all these long months
wasted it is still raining.

LIVED A LIE

Do I miss the cold breeze from the winter hour
or do I miss the warm touch
that turned my heart so sour.

Did I live this past
or am I living the past in present.
Am I still dreaming or did I wake up,
am I following the truth or am I following
the lies now that the summer hour dies.

MOTHER BAND
for my mom—Naile Aksoy

Speaks the words of truth
teaches the right from wrong
because in her love is strong.

Disciplines from experience
does not want to see another heart cry
does not want laughter over another's tears,
oh...what a job she bears.

No one knows of a friend
every friend has betrayed a friend
everybody has given up on each other
and we believe we are alone
but there is someone there
second from a guardian angel...

Mother…
always there, through good times and bad
through tough times and easy
through rain or sunshine
always there to hold your hand
because she holds the mother band.

STRANGER

Passes by like a wind, afraid to be seen,
following the cold shadows left behind, where I freeze,
through that long lost look, I find no warmth
through the spoken words, I find no peace,
cuts through my heart like a weapon to kill,
I bleed with anger; he laughs at what he has done;
does not care when I call for help,
looks away when I reach.

Looks at me, like looking at dirt,
asks for a meaningless hug,
Through the eyes, I see pain
but he does not know that what he has done,
one day it will all bring him rain,
that will leave him never like a lying stain.

Promises a future,
yet in his heart there lies no future,
apologises for empty words,
yet in his words there is no sorry.

After all that was said and done,
he does not recall the importance of a past,
walks away into the dark clouds of hell,
becoming a stranger to me overtime;

loses himself between lies and betrayal,
does not remember the importance of respect,
plays against the truth of it all.

Where he is; he creates,
where he leaves; he destroys,
where he walks; he betrays,
what he speaks; he lies
what he laughs; he playd a fool.

After all this time wasted,
when I thought I knew truth,
I only knew someone that did not exist,
cause now you are a stranger to me,
a stranger I do not want to
be related to

LOOKING BACK
for Dad—rest in peace

The windiest ocean and the highest mountain,
may steal our reach,
The darkest night and the worst blizzard
may steal our sight.,
but there is nothing in the world that can ease the
Pain that lies in my heart.
My heart calls out for you but
the ruby of the snow hides you,
your image is warmth to my heart that melts the snow,
even thow there are many miles between our reach,
It makes us both think, feel and talk to each other without
our presence.
We had a love that began when I was born,
time went by and days slowly faded away til there come a

day when things were not the same,
I know deep inside that my love was to blame,
for trusting in you so quick
that you are here to stay
I look back through the day you left
I could not make up a thing that was real.
I look back and remember all the tears I cried when you
did not wake up,
I look back and remember how you did not want to listen
to what I had to say,
I remember how you gave me comfort
just so you could rest
I look back and remember your smile that made me
laugh,
your touch that was so gentle, but cold
All that is left are memories,
even thow you may not realize it,
just your memory makes me love you deeper every time.
When I one day clear my feelings, I will look back and
always remember what a special father you were.

SPECIAL

Stands there,
I see but I am too scared to say a thing
acting as I did not see,
I hear a melody
the way you called my name is music to my ears.
I turn back and that is when like a spark I felt a bond
growing inside of me.
You came as if no one ever mattered to you but me,
your soft look is heaven to me,
your deep brown eyes brightens my presence.
It all seemed like a dream, but this time it was real.
You cared more than your soul was meant to care,

only you see me the way I am,
only you see how special I can be.
You make me blossom in a yard full of roses,
yet I am the dusty dried one amoung all the others,
you see me clear and you choose me among all other
beauty.
A tear of happines rolls down my cheek,
you tell me you'll be there,
you tell me how much I mean to you simply by standing
there.
You show me how much you care, simply by explaining
things.
I ask myself…how does life treat me?
How could life go on without you?
Where I think, I cannot handle the thought of losing you.
If I ever do, I will then lose a part of my heart,
and I will be left with nothing to beat our special
friendship.
You open the doors to heaven and help me walk in,
while others drag me out and surround me with evil.
You made me realize how special I am,
just by being there,
which makes you so special to me in every way.

FEELINGS MUST DIE

That is it,
I never thought I would ever come to this point;
the point of needing to let go
being forced by your actions to let go of my inner
feelings
my tears well up in my eyes when I feel your need;
you do not care.

I see you there but..
when I talk, I speak to myself,
when I smile, I laugh on my own,
nothing I say makes a difference anymore
you do not want to listen
you do not want to hear
you do not want to see
all the things you promised you would.

Memories haunt me
I knew your dark reflection
I heard your lies
I listened to your steps
now I listen to echos
when feelings
must die.

LIFE AND WIND

Life is like the wind
when wind is life

THE BEAUTY FROM THE LIGHT

Fresh breeze of spring calls for my heart,
the clouds so gray, I wish I could see.
From afar I see light
its brightness guides me towards it
where I feel safe.

I feel warmth, I do not know how
I see heaven, I do not know where I am
I am given breath through softness
beauty lies in me, through a mirror I can not see.

REFLECTIONS

The words I speak are the lips you owned
The laughter I laugh is the smile you shared
The pain I suffer is the person you are.

I miss what never existed of you
through your lies
blinded to my own shadow.

Whenever I reached
further it reflected back
closer I got
slowly you faded away.

WHAT TOMB OF LOVE

What can I say
Beauty is the tomb
when I do not have the words to speak,
of life
What can I feel
where it receives
when nothing is touched,
dying love.
where can I go
when no directions are given
where can I stay
when they all leave
where can I cry
when past kills my future
where can I fly
when I want to get away
what happens when life is betrayed.

WHERE WE DIED

Passing by the tomb
where our meeting has been destroyed
where lies took over life
turned precious things into dust.

I breathe memories
where I stood
I watched things die
when I understood each lie.

Tears welled up in my eyes
a stranger to my heart,
a snake to my soul,
a loser to my mind.

THE CLOUD

Distance is the journey
I cannot reach
Love is the cloud
I cannot touch.

THINK OF YOU

Where did you leave us that November afternoon?
How did you forget all that you won?
Where I stand
I do not know where to go
where I sit
I do not know when to get up
where I laugh
I do not know why
where I cry

I think of you.

HAND IN HAND

The words you speak
completes the sentence I say
the smile you share
is the laughter I laugh.

Like two curving lines
almost similar
but same
symbol of truth
speaks our name.

When we reach
heaven opens up
where we stand
the world shows beauty.

Through this happines found
we leave our past behind
because when we get together
our hearts held hand in hand.

YOU DISAPPEARED

You come for my direction
I walked
you ran
I ran
you left
I leave
you disappear.

CLOUD

Through a window corner
I can see it
Among blooming flowers
I can sense it
between million streets
I lose it.

HELL

Took me to heaven
it was a beautiful place
lightened by love
touched by life.

When I woke up
the light was shut
and feelings gone
left a shadow with no identity
where I realized
I was in hell.

TREASURE

Killed my feelings for beauty
adjusted in my tomb for
your comfort
When one you killed
is me
holding the truth of love
in the future's treasure.

SIT ALONE

Trust is the weapon
against your own feelings,
Hate is the future love
to your heart.

When you cry
you may never laugh again
when you walk
they all walk with you
when you sit
you sit alone.

OUR ART

Traveling through a web of colours
dark and light
with every touch of red,
I include your image
afraid to lose what use to be.
The mixing of two hearts,
two shades and souls
the rainbow of us melts down the brush
and spill down the art of love.
Just a touch of reach;
we move further apart,
just a ear away from each other's voice
we break through quietness into loudness
where feelings cannot be heard.
Every tear that rolls down my face,
the image of you and me is easily taken away by fear
replacing memories with blank thoughts
taking us further to a future away from one another.

GONE

Like the doors of heaven
I open up my heart to you.
Walking by a cloud
I do not know if it is love I see
because the closer this cloud gets
it slowly fades away.
Following the last touch of your shadow
leading me towards a garden of roses
where I become the seed of your love.
In the air I melt and see your reflection,
I hear a melody, it is music to my ears
I feel warmth, it is your touch
I see happiness, it is your smile
I wake up, you are gone.

FUTURE

Traveling through a web of colours,
afraid to lose you by the blink of my eye,
afraid to lose the shade of your love,
the mixing of you and me,
the rainbow of our future melts.

IN SO MANY....

In so many words that are hidden
reveal my feelings,
in so many actions that are made
reveal all I do for you,
in so many stories that are shared
reveal my need,
in so many calls

reveal how much I think of you,
in so many poems that are written
reveal the journey of this love,
in so many songs that are sung
reveal your character,
in so many thoughts
reveal my love for you that starts
from the bottom of my heart.

MASK

In the paradise of hearts left bare
inside my mind
I heard his thoughts
a voice calling my name
mistaken by the echo of another face.
When he speaks
I feel his pain
when he laughs
I cry
within him is
a masked emotion
caring yet not revealed.
Divulges of the details
of what use to be.
As he lives
slowly a part dies
when goes without discovery
as this face lives
hiding answers
to questions that are scared
to surface.

She understands him not
for his thoughts

but for what she sees
which is merely a mask
that she has confused
that will be lifted one day
to reveal all that she has avoided
when I missed….

SAW LOVE'S TRUTH DIE

Moved on with his lonely cry
searching for a piece of heaven
through his tears
I see river
and feel his pain.

They were in love
when silence spoke
they become alone
so long waited
for a tomorrow
feelings were gone.

Stuck in the middle
of a restless heart
as they live on
each is searching
for answers
not yet
questioned.

I witnessed heart's truth
slowly die.

COME TRUE

Dreams are not
just for hope
but to come true.

FADED

Life shifts positions
mistaken by the shadow left alone
with its eyes
opened up my own
with the smile
brightened all living darkness.

Willingly opened up my heart
taught it to forget
spread around piece of itself
surrounded me with love
becoming the seed
of its perfection.

When storm broke down
we both saw above
feelings become blurry
everything faded away.

HER NAME

Speaks his shadow
follows what he sees
laughs when she laughs
cries when she cries.

What he hides

kills him inside

Within him I see truth
yet afraid of what is real

Like the wind
blown place to place
by the echos of her trace

As I listen
I feel his pain
when he laughs
I cry his rain
when he speaks
I die
when her name
we dwell
I watch their love swell.

ONE OF A KIND

Your words do not leave my lips
Your touch does not leave my skin
Your look does not leave my beauty
your promises do not leave my mind
because you are one of a kind.

ROAD

There are times when we need to let go
times when two roads never meet
two hearts don't make a whole
and everything you wish you could find
never reaches the palm of your hand
that is when we dream a little bit longer

and a step further to discover
what is really meant to be.
It might not always be easy not to feel
and it might not always be easy to leave
who you love behind
and watch your own dreams fade
But that is when we must feel tears
and feel pain
to find the answer to what life is all about.

Behind each tear there is beauty
hiding for your happiness
What you don't have and
what you would never think about
comes your way
opens up your eyes
blinded by its beauty.
Feelings you never felt
the touch you never reached
the sun that never gave you warmth
takes you to the true love
that you thought you felt before
but this time the road is clear
the roads meet as one
and the hearts beat as one
together you feel as one
because the road to love has just begun.

TIL YOU FIND

When you feel you have it all
you just lost it
When you know you may never feel
you gain it all
By the time you know it is tears that you cry

you're in pain

Through the clouds in the sky
and the mountain so high
you find your dream
but you cannot reach,
through the river you walk
when you reach the top
you may never talk.

Feelings get shattered
hearts get torn in pieces
memories forgotten
promises broken
nothing is used as a token...

We know this dream
was never meant to be
shortened by life's best gifts
that hurt but ease overtime
until one day you realize
what you really dreamt of
is what you just found.

MASKED EMOTIONS I SEE

Bound between clouds
misled by the sky's dark clouds
when he reaches for the sun,
lost between the darkness of the night
comes fairly towards my distance
confused and out of light,
torn between two livings
creates roads among long rivers.

In him lies true dreams
mistaken by reality and fantasy
feelings masked
as emotions age young love.

What I can't see
through his dreamy eyes I feel
what I can't hear
through his soft spoken words I tear.

What I say
meaning does not explain
what I do
thank you is complain.

GUARDIAN SISTER
for Renate Ursula Aksoy

Through a mirror corner
I see what I am
I feel what I feel
I speak what I speak
it is myself in flesh and blood
yet it is someone else
equal but different
When I cry
it wipes my tears
and gives me laughter
shines a light on my beauty
when it is dark
when I am about to fall
protects me from it all.

When I laugh
the mirror reflects back

reaches for my hand
whispers to me softly
"....I am your guardian sister...."
Then I know I am safe.

The mirror I do not need to glance at
to see someone like me
because here stands a sister
living exactly like me.

WONDER
for Dad—rest in peace

Where would I be, if you were around
where would I go, if you guided my road
how would I look if heaven never took
would my life be an open book?....

Lies there
million miles away
resting but full of betray
ignores me when I visit
does not hear when I speak
does not see when I peek.

When I reach he moves away
when I cry he asks me to leave
when I call he wants me to forget
Why did you leave me?
Why is the tomb a better place?
Why did you not think that one day
I would wonder what went wrong?

Left without a second thought
did not even remember

to leave a part of a thank you.

REACH FOR HEAVEN

Never pick up the petals of a rose
if the rose lost its stem
Never try to find the root
if the the rose has no living.

Never trust the sun that seems out of reach
they are always the ones nearest to the heart.
When you try a little harder
and follow your heart a little bit closer
the doors to heaven will open up a little bit closer.

ROSE AMONG ALL FLOWERS

Sometimes it is very hard to choose
the rose among all flowers
it blooms there for mind's attention.

Reaches for your arms to be held;
when you pick it up
it loses its beauty,
becomes like the other
yet like a stranger.

The root remains in place
for memories to trace
petals blown side to side
that is when feelings we must hide.

NEVER MEET
for Dad—rest in peace

Where can I go to see you?
Where can I sit to hear you?
Where do I run to hold you?
When you left me no directions
to trace you.

Why did you hurry to get away?
Why did heaven not let you stay?
How do you lie there so peaceful
yet full of betrayal?

Why do I miss you?
When I don't know you
Why do I try to reach you when
through the clouds of heaven you are hiding
Why do I cry for someone
I never met?

NOT THERE

Looking down the window corner,
longing for a past
to come again.
When feelings sweep through my soul
making the heart so cold,
and only lost love remains
searching for missing pieces.
The heart is compared to flowers
but unlike it
because the flower does not wait
for the wind to give life,
so it can love again.

A key was given to enter greater love
steps on the flowers to reach
that is when I still knock to be heard again
to reach back the source of dreams
that are not there.

PAST DIED

Past,
thought to be true
through the heart of truth
I look upon you.
Through the eyes
the painting I lived
thousand miles away I saw laughter
when I experienced pain
I heard a melody
that was my cry
afraid of an image yet not there,
calls out for my soul
I wish I were deaf
I see the smile
I wish I were blind
when I feel the touch
I wish I died.

HIS PAIN

In the paradise of hearts left bare
inside my mind
I heard his thoughts
a voice calling out my name
mistaken by the echo of another face.

As he speaks

I feel pain
when he laughs
I cry.

Within him is a masked emotion
carefree, yet not revealed
divulges of the details of what use to be.

As he lives,
slowly lets a part die
as it leaves without discovery.

Lies a woman
holding the answers to questions
that are scared to surface.
She understands him not for his thoughts
but what she sees
which is merely a mask
that will be lifted one day
to reveal all that he is
that she has avoided.
....again both will lose someone they never
realized existed because this love is a chain.

ARMS OF LIGHT

Alone by the burning fireplace
I drift off...holding a seed
everything becomes cloudy
soon dark.

In the cold shadows of sleep
caught in the middle of fear
striving for a place to belong,
screaming from the top of
my lungs
but no one wants to hear me
and I am cut off.

Only an echo like my own replies,
away from me
at the light of living care,
held me tightly from afar
to never fear,
to never doubt myself
where being held made me
feel safe;
being alone in the arms of light.

That lonely seed
grew into a rose
but soon I woke up
and everything faded away
into the dark clouds of living betrayal.

CLOSE MY EYES AT LAST

I see clouds, the rain is my cry,
With every tear a part of me dies without discovery.
All images, freezes the wave created with guilt
Arrogance with no dreams to save this bleeding heart.
Inside of me lies welled up feelings
searching for profound happiness,
But all it can find is warmth,
like a portal to a dimension of which
I could not reach.
As I stared through the window,
tears falling gently in couples,
Adding to the layers of cold fluff on the window still.
I nestled into the corner
between the wall of the window and
a wall that slightly protruded from the house,
Thoughts brought me back to the times
when you were the only thing
That kept me sane, when in a moment's time,
I thought I found the key to my heart,
A cold wind swept me back to reality
into the present love that is my rain.
I shivered and rubbed my hands together
as I did not want to believe
what is now out of reach.
Like a blink of an eye you faded away
through my own reflection radiating
through the window,
sitting like solitary and insignificant
figures on the wrong side of the window,
opposite of what the heart use
to be.

SOAP

sitting there...
plastered with scum,
so little of who you are
is forever on that dish.

Clinging to dirt
you stay in big bubbles,
when you I hold
to rinse
little by little you slip away.

I watch the drain eat the water
with your flesh,
bit by bit
you disappear
before my eyes
too bad my hands were wet
and I was holding the soap side of you.

20 YEARS

A melody brought back a memory
a place brought back a smile,
a mirror brought back a tear
I hadn't felt before.

A number brought back sadness
a cloud brought back a fear
that if I lost all
I'd forget the last 20 years of me.

A GIFT

I was going to pick some flowers
to show how I feel
but when I got there
the yard was hard and frozen
and there were no flowers around.

POSTMORTEM

I heard the knell,
it's signal irk to my ears.
Through a shaded area
blinded to the ray of light,
where I absorb a bound of knives
and cut myself away.

Your voice like a signal to disaster,
pushing and pulling me further
to a place I longed not til
my years be yours.

You fade away into the darkness
of my life,
melody of your voice
gone
into the whispers of night,
you had turned your back,

and I am following

HIS PAST

Through his steps,
there is a part that he is longing for.
A part that may have come unexpectedly
and now that part remains not whole
that can fulfill his hope.

There remains a tear in the past
that brings it to life overtime,
that when he passes by a reflecting glass
he walks away.

The cry of a child echoes back memories
I do not know if this brings him joy
or simply a reminder of a past he left behind.

Little of his joy and pain
I sense inside
as if I bring back a past that
clouds his life today.

FROM AFAR

Close by the door he pause to stand
I can't help thinking whether my life I should doubt.
Through the cold air he stands underneath,
my soul shivers,
looks ahead and away when someone passes
as if he is longing for a friend;
when he sees what he adores
he stops to stare.

From afar, I watch him
there are hidden tears welled up in his eyes
as if they been from a past,
by the gloom of his face; I vision sadness,
lost sadness
or a happiness that was never given,
I wonder where his share went?!

From the reflecting mirror behind him
I sense little of his childhood,
something he was not given credit for
that he carries til today
and doubts himself to new chances
that may offer him his dreams.

From afar, I watch him laugh
as he is talking on the phone
as if million stars surrounded him this moment;
he must have been talking to someone
that truly brings out his smile.

Watching the way he moves his lips
when he talks,
spoke to me of his gentle personality

that is often hidden.

From afar, I watch him go for a cup of water
as if he is trying to wash away his years,
that made him wiser and stronger
that I long to be.

From afar, he draws me into thoughts,
I must get closer,
the force of life
I can not help feeling indebted
to whom I sense his feelings.

For me to sense and walk away
would be betrayal and ignorance
that I go through.

From afar, I walk towards him
through crowds
as I get closer
I lose him through thought
and he becomes a reminder of how I feel.

DESTROYED MEMORIES!

When life seems to shift into positions, every step into
closer love,
seems to fade away; little by little, step by step, making
the heart so cold.
With every thought of you, a part of me dies without
discovery, with every
dream I see no future, just taunting images of what used
to be, all
feelings so innocent yet burned alive, with every soul
shared, rain is

the sensation, just like leaving the flower die in the cold without a second thought.

A heart torn in pieces by the light that guided me through living, but now I

wake up from a dream of what used to be, and losing the wings to fly.

Inside of me lies a part just a million miles away whispering my name,

with every sound it makes my heart bleed with torture.

All memories now burned alive into ashes of pain where in every ash lies

laughter, pleasure, and hearts all vanished and gone. Trying to look down the truth, hoping for you to come back to stop the flame that destroys

eternity. But with every whisper that I pray—isolation destroys. Trying to look into a different mirror, yet all I see reflects what it already seen.

LOOK FOR YOUR STAR...YOU ARE NEVER ALONE

Look up at the sky
among a thousand stars,
one must have glanced at you.

Put all of your trust in that star,
let its light be eyes to yours.

Learn to shine like that star
let its beauty take you high.

Stars have a million friends
they are all with you all the time.

All you have to do is look up

and believe in your true friends.
You will then find
you are never alone.

DEAD

Childhood come…
Walked away from that
leaving me lonely
among a crowded world.

You took with you my fantasy
leaving me reality,
in it, I miss the most…
is the dead that you become.

MYSTERY MAN

There must have been something
to make the gentleness of this face hideous,
the eyes so weak as if he was to cry,
hiding a lost sadness in a present smile of act;
trying to fit in a world of profession
realizing not that just by standing here
night is turned into day

There must have been something
to turn his loving heart against all living,
respecting the outer rather than the inner that
he blinds himself to.

There must have been something
to a man of looks to doubt himself to it,
needing comfort from an opposite attraction,
unaware that his eyes all beauty shine,

his smile; stars are brought to daylight.

There must have been something
to make this gentle, loving, sensitive man a mystery.

**THERE IS NO ONE TO BLAME...HE WRITES,
TO SHARE MY LONELINESS.**

Dignity and patience kept them apart,
a mother has no longer a place in touching
her young man's heart.

Locked in a unsolved madness
on a fall afternoon,
he committed the unbeliveable

Now he has gone a long way
through the past,
he can not know
in what familiar patterns
the long years would have gone.

Roses will ripen
leaves will colour and fall,
season after season
the good and bad will pass,
century after century
time will lay away
for golden times to come
that he did not stay to find.

Another loved one missed
by the world
that is left to rest once and for all
alone.

NO MORE

Feels like another rainy day...
a rose petal falls
where a tear of blood spills
and soft water sheds them together,
along they mix
only to create the unrenewable.

The sky swirls and hurls,
yet the sounds wander down to find
a place to fit in...
others not to belong!

A soulable mixture created,
the blood that never dries
as always:
time constructs pain,
only now there is no more of the rose.

AS SWEET AS IT MAY BE, IT'S AS SOUR AS ANYTHING CAN BE.

A letter
a word
a sentence
said of care
if not passed to the mouth
from the heart;
its sweetness stinks.

A tale
a story
a poem
said of love

if not passed through the heart
its feeling one of lies.

The tongue,
the centre piece of the mouth..
tastes and feels and moves
as it creates different tones and languages.

With every word said;
as sweet as it may sound,
its meaning is as sour as anything can ever be.

ALL OF STRENGTH ... POWERED BY WEAKNESS

Her eyes had the golden stars shining through them,
now she can barely keep them open.
Her smile gave warmth to the coldest days,
now she barely feels like sunshine.
Her head up high; never rude
now she barely wakes up.
Her strength one of a man
now she is barely the woman she is.

When inner beauty reflects through
an awaiting evil eye simply reflects back,
like thunder on a stormy night;
wakening the soul and mind
tearing everyone involving hearts
right from the back of their ribs
making it difficult not to give up.

What is the mirror
that reflects the outside beauty
for others to eye wrong.

What is the reflecting of that mirror
when ill and its strength
powered by weakness.

WHEN I MISS IT MOST

Tell me
where I left all fantasy;
the playful thoughts,
carried no pain.

The kiss given where
it hurt the most
and healed a wounded scar.

Tell me
where did reality start with us?
When playful thoughts
only seek own advantage
and a kiss brings pain.
Childhood just died
and now I miss it most.

HALF WAY...TIL YOU COME

Far away...
above the mountains high
climbing to reach,
I slip from the ice and snow
invisible to the eye.

Half way up where my heart lies
frozen to any feeling
with no movement,
cold thoughts in my head remind me,

I will be alone once again.

Half way between sea and sky
neither with me to belong,
neither high nor low
I will reach you
even if I tried.

I will sit here half way
between heaven and earth
waiting til you come.

STAR IN THE NIGHT

In the dark...
outside the bedroom window
glance at thy soul,
reach for the bottom of my heart,
grab it like the force of power
as you make it understand
the sweet dreams to come.

Translate all of fears
into bits of love
longing to be put together
like the star in the night.

MY FATHER
for Dad—rest in peace

Blow away the wind from my wet eyes
send me an angel from heaven to rescue me
give me back my happiness to find life again.

Bend over and let me feel your presence near me

reach out your hand and move me closer to your
gentleness
so that I may know you are near.

Forget me not,
I worship you
try to understand and forgive my mistakes
rescue me from fear

One day I will meet you
that day everything will be right
life and luck will be one
and everything that is hard and painful
will vanish away forever.

Wake me up from my cry of loneliness,
wake me from the pain in me that kills my inside
where I am ashamed of what I feel.

Come to me, whisper in my ear,
"I am with you, I will help you, and love you"
I know you are near me.
Yet I am in a world of sinners.

I am longing for the day I will finally meet you
and be able to sit beside you forever and never feel
lonely.

SIMPLY STILL

Through a drawn mirror
I stand not alone to the beauty
of that heart
but among other to be judged
and taken as a fool once again.

Take not thy hand
that is unheld by the power of you,
share not thy words
that speak temporary sympathy
because this profound picture is simply still.

THE ANGEL IN MY DREAM

Living through life's rainbow,
I see all coming forth with different meaning,
Leaving its final feeling for me to live.
Walking by the shadows of the past,
Darkness falls behind while a
sweet melody come racing through.
From a distance, I saw a flaring light
and a shadowed figure
embedded in a soft bluish-white look.
It soon come closer then faded away.
A tear trickled down my cheek,
this heaven's sweet angel come forth
to ask if there were something he could seek.
From his fall breeze, I become colour blind to all that
lives and breathes.
He comes at me with force, tears down the wall with
temporary care.
He clutches at my soul and rushes it with his gentle
hands,
carries me off my feet and guides them through the steps
of his dance.
He slaps me in the face leaving it damp with temporary
joy, every living
rule rushes past my ears blocking out the sounds and
people of woe.
He whispers to me softly confusing promise of hope, it
takes control of my

mind and brings the depressing thoughts aside.
He gives me breath, pulls out a hibernated cry for help,
he opens up my heart, teaches it to beat,
he opens up my arms, and teaches them to embrace,
Rushes through my whole, needing its invitation to live;
soon he took me by the hand, let's me lead the dance, opens up my eyes with
his own and gives me back my chance. That's when I woke up from a dream!

RAINBOW OF LIFE

Looking at the rainbow of life, I see all coming forth with different meaning leaving its final feelings.
Taunting images of all that used to be, with every shade,
I found the beginning to a dream that soon found its way to the end without a second thought.
Every colour symbolizes what used to be, traces of every shade spill
down my soul, turning all my tears into the blackest night.
With every step of truth, inside a sin was far ahead, where evil
drags into the wrong way, which makes love so innocent fade away
into growing flames of pain.
When heaven finds its love inside, within and alone,
without the need of a shoulder, yet the need of that special touch that engraves love into a heart.
When every need is out of reach,
When every laughter is the cry,
when every touch is a fool's,

messages of life's rainbow are sent, the force of living its
different shades into different meanings to all different
hearts,
like a web of rainbows, each rainbow's heart is attached
to a different colour
leading life into different pains making up a life.

LIGHT

Tears come to my eyes as I looked into the window,
the rain had just fallen as a sigh of the future.
I could see the warmth that was once present,
but I must not feel it.
I sense a sweet melody but I try not to hear it.
It is like looking at a portal to a dimension of which I
could not reach.
For a moment I had found profound happiness radiating
through
my life, but soon I had to hide the true feelings and
look into a different mirror, yet like looking at what I
already
seen haunting me.
When Images of the light you once brought to me come
taunting
back to my mind.
When in the night at the forest of words when I panicked,
every step took me into thicker darkness,
when the only way out, was when you brought me light
and called me to silence.
Now we lie apart at night in the forest of fear,
when I am afraid we won't hear each other over clattering
branches,
over both our voices calling,
In winter when we are both apart in the hour,
the sun runs liquid then freezes,

caught in the mantilla of empty trees,
my heart listens to empty words I can not hear,
through the cold stethoscope of fear,
A voice in my head reminds me, what the light teaches.
Slowly you translate fear into love,
then you leave me without a second thought.

CHILD
·for Jason Balaci

He opens up his eyes,
his presence is a present to the world,
he speaks but it has no meaning,
he cries to be understood.
Skin so soft, like the petals of a rose,
His smile filled with pure joy
in him there is purity
no thoughts or troubles.
Unique and one of a kind,
growing older day by day
each time experiencing life.
I gaze through his eyes, thinking,
what a precious thing!
What a better friend one could have than
a child, so trustful and pure hearted.
I wish I could explain to him
what life is all about
I wish he would understand me when I say
that you only get one chance to do extraordinary
things, so do it right and to the fullest.
A child, the happiness of love,
cries when he sees the world cry,
because his is the answer to love and
the only true friend.

DARKNESS

She says that the sun shines,
but he sees the sky's dark clouds
She tells him that summertime gives warmth,
but he shivers in a cold breeze.
She says the flowers smell good
yet he does not see them in the snow and ice,
she takes off her clothes
and swims through the beach,
he puts on his coat and goes
slowly over the ice.

LITTLE ROSE...

You found a little rose...
young and fresh
you picked it from its root
with force,
held it in your hand
bent it between your fingers
until you ruined it.
You slowly force it away
bit by bit
til it had no more life,
you let go of the bits and pieces
on the ground beside thy feet
then you stood up and left
almost stepping on the dead
not even realizing it
You little rose...it was me.

THE LETTER

I ask of you one thing
to agree and respect
thy decisions.

Every year I look back
finding the best in me
as I change for the better
and work closer towards happiness.

If there was really a part
that cared for thy feelings truly
I ask that my existence
be taken off your mind
as death may do
when pain we no longer can stand.

This our knowledge
lies not in a future
of a cup of coffee
that forgiveness speaks in
thy sorrow
destroying all of memories.

Kill thy feelings
what ever loss may be
let all of gain be given away
because after this
I no longer
want to stay.

FUNERAL

Bring me no more laughter
that our beginning showed
bring me no more joy
that your care brought
bring me no red roses
that thy kiss spoke
bring me no promises
that lies never trust
bring me no coffee
that our future broke
bring me nothing of you
that broke thy heart
right from the start.

"...SEE YOU AT THE FUNERAL..."

You'll see me sure,
inside thy casket you think
among the dead you think to you
I will speak
in white clothes
you'll see me not
surrounded by flowers for the dead
I will not lie
because you think
in my spoken words
I just said
Good-bye.

THE REFLECTING GLASS

Through a mirror
I watch her as
she stands pensively,
through her eyes
lost in time
forgotten deep below
betrayal
of an unknown angel.

Hurt by what the world
has proven to be,
confused by the truth
she trembles
as she creates lies and lives them
at the same time.

From a reflecting glass
I cry her tears
at the same hour
trying to comfort her loss.

She understands not
the goodness of this loss
and its ended gain
but just what never existed.

In the meantime
she will stand across
from me reflecting back
who I am.

ALONE

Lost in time
date with no number
among loneliness
thy eyes caught sight
I become no longer one
but a part of two ones.

Slowly the breath I breathe
another life given to me
I am no longer alone
but two as one.

Walked above the world
through a glass door
spark in my heart
like never before
heart taking over the mind
that is why now…
alone again I stand.

SPEAK TO ME

Speak to me
take another shot on
tearing my heart from
behind my ribs.

Prove that you won
when you mixed
two hearts
like salt and sugar
turning something so sweet
into something so sour.

Turn the warmth of that endless spark
into settling smoke
that fills my body to ache.

Speak to me,
look at what you've done
tell me
how did my truth do you wrong?

Why are all the lies
still not proof to me
that I must become strong—
Speak to me!

WARMTH OF SHYNESS

Cold winds on that Sunday afternoon
work aside for rest to bring the hour
the illness of a young woman;
shyness acts her personality.

Riding along the stop lights
as she frowns and asks within
"tremble not thy stomach
speak not of the heart
that this world truth not take,
my month has brought its illness
that the lips must seal its cause.."

Let not my weakness
bring the speech of a brother
to a sister
that a young woman cannot bear
but the words within this brother
speak the inside

that freezes a young woman into stare.

Her pale cheekbones
blushed by the warmth of shyness
that the words of a man created
makes her wish for a place to run
and to never be found.

What he spoke
are said to be the words of his knowledge
he might be right,
maybe so wrong
but he does not let the sweet talk of a
chocolate fool his business.\Dedicated to "the brother"

TWIXTER

Must say..
this life must ask for something
when someone comes with care,
the world must need something to prove
when of me someone decides to approve.

Just walked out of the dark
gray clouds of hell;
please let me stay
where I now choose to sit
let me choose my own destination
let me calm that burning pain
that hell took me for a train.

Leave me..
walk away before
I become another drop of
falling rain

let me go on alone
my eyes need the sleep of years,
my feet need the rest of a lifetime
to heal
because my right
the past decided to steal.

THEY

They may speak
I may hear
they may know
I may understand
they may care
I may not dare.

DID NOT MEAN

Did not mean to repeat
my pain on you
did not mean to rub
the mistakes of another
on you
but my heart is wounded
that it needs to heal
for today
because I decided to give up
on tomorrow.

Did not mean to say good-bye
but something inside
needs you not to stay
because I do not need another
with my heart to play.

MISERY

Lived misery
tasted misery
talked to misery
cried for misery
healed misery
but what did I gain
rather than itself
…misery.

LOVE'S TASK

One day
we will realize
this hate and betrayal
is getting us no where
but sadly no one will be left
to finally understand
that love does not harm
but brings us life.

SO THEY TELL ME

They tell me
I can do it all over again
but it will not be the same
they do not understand
I want the old
rather then the new.

I know chances come once in life
and may not always choose to stay
but feelings remain of what used to be.
The heart is no part of the mind

they do not realize I can not separate
the heart from the mind
that caused me all of sorrow....

SUN AT WINTER

The sun is shining on a winter day
flowers growing in the snow
as the sky glitters like million diamonds.
Roads are slippery on a summer dream
where I walk towards
and become nothing but misery.

Life is a rocky road
never promises best
traveling through it
where the special is sorrow
and the sorrow is special
everyone must ride
but no one will understand
why the sun is shining on a winter day...

There is no sun on a winter day
there is
yet there can't be
there was none
right from the start
because I am the sun
when you are winter.

CALL

Hang up
as much as you wish
it is not

my heart
that will later itch.

IF I WAS HER

No longer
am I an angel
that every one has been
no longer am I a star that
everyone has been.

They took my mind
They took my soul
left my heart
to stroll

left…

as you become another
if I was her
I would never bother.

SOLVED

It's okay
it's all right
it's no problem
not to worry
not to cry
I'll
be just fine
now that I don't have to try.

DIPT

Passing by like the wind
on a cold January day,
the scent of a new beginning
shivers the heart,
Stands there
known by the unknown,
unknown by the known,
the beauty from the sky
falls into your eyes
you glitter into a million diamonds
that fall into my eyes

REGRET

As much as I did not
want to say good-bye
I must
as much as I did not
want to leave
I did
as much as I did not
want to fight
I acted
as much as I did not
want to hate
I do
as much as I did not want to care
I loved
as much as I did not
want to know
I have and regret.

YOUR TIME

Dreams are needs
hopes full of faith
times full of waiting
until everybody is sitting
and you are standing.

MISERY BECOMES NOTHING

Misery only loses
nothing of it becomes
your winner
misery only harms
nothing of it becomes
your health
misery only hates
nothing of it becomes
your love.

STARS TO FORGET

The eyes
fooled by the stars in the sky
with a blink you caught
every sparkle
and willingly brought it
to my heart.

Days become short to end
Sleep was just another
forgotten chore
that I did not want to do
because knowing I have you
every living thing is left behind.

Soon I taught myself
to forget
that now what I cherished
I must turn my back and regret.

PICTURE DREAM

Slight sight at a picture
I started to dream
fantasizing off reality
holding the unreachable
more like someone I did not know
Something hard had hit me
no words can describe the feeling
within this fullfilled heart,
it sure felt true
yet I wake up from a daydream
holding not the shadow of a dream
but a photo with colours that beam.
There it came
closer than ever before
I still thought I was in the middle
of a daydream
when the photo turned to you
I become frightend by the echos of another face
so turned away .
Something remained unfolded
as days started to turn sour
time becomes difficult
roads must be choosen
someone must be left behind
but who?
Each minute
came closer to an end

soon you slipped away
when I became
frightened to stay
so I choose you to betray.
I know I hurt the innocence
but choices of innocence
lie within me too
it did not matter if I called or not
I did not want to hear what you've become
but wanted you to slip away bit by bit
not giving the heart a chance.
Sorry...!

ROSE OF LOVE

Like the blooming of a rose
love giving so much life
through the window corner
I watch it bloom when
the sun shines

Opens up so beautiful
nothing can stop my needing future
as I watch it slowly
being created.

Crawling through a web of thoughts
I wonder where you are
blinked....as I awaken from a dream
looking out the window
where the rose of love died.

WINDOW

tears well up in my eyes
as I look out the window
the rain falls,
washes away people I avoided
hiding feelings as I look into a
different mirror
wishing all would hate
rather than care.
When I become forced to let a part die
without a chance.
With each rain drop and tear
I leave behind a piece of myself
I hear the rainstorm
in the middle of my cry
while a sweet melody
comes healing
to the heart.
A tear trickled down my cheek
my heart I can no longer feel
the warmth brought
life.
For a moment...
profound happiness radiated
through me
I envisioned myself through the beauty
of it all,
I lost all my senses
imagined all that love had to offer
the bliss lasted for only a few seconds
before reality broke the dream.
It was there
like a portal to a dimension
I must have

images made me feel sorry for myself
knowing if I only tried harder not to wake up
I would be able to reach heaven
through the dark clouds in living hell.
If only you were real
if only you stayed near
I would not have to stand on this side
of the window and cry.

ENDLESS SEA

Walking by life's clouds
leaving behind the rain
from a distance
a soft blue-green
figure appears
the answer to a dream
bringing about intense beauty,

my eyes blinded to all it sees
I hear the unspoken words passed to me
through the beauty of the smile
melts the ice in me
the touch so gentle
makes a dream come alive
pure energy
stopped me and held me
in his trance.

Every kiss
casts a deeper spell
slowly translates fear into love
waves rolling over me
I feel the sea
the body floating next to mine

sand forces passion
when fears come
washing over
deep inside we die
vision had taken me to the brightest
living on an endless sea.

THE PARKER

She stands arms
akimbo!
Frozen in her thoughts
deep dark black pools
are her eyes in a dead stare
it's never warm...

FLOWERS THEY DIE

In the paradise of hearts left bare
surrounded by the river blue
among blooming flowers,
when the sun shines through
the sand giving a million directions
all aside staring at the coming fall
through the window corner
watching leaves being blown to
a place like never before
the fresh air breathes beautifully
soft mellow sound from the wind
I blinked to find a leaf being sent to
me from heaven
carrying the face of a long known stranger.

With the eyes
held me closely

with the touch
gave me warmth
with the kiss
gave me breath
with the spoken words
cleared away my past.

THE CLOSED DOORS

Friday wakes me up
with a heart so tight;
soft breeze
strangles all of living veins...

the ringing of a phone
so strange,
so unexpectedly
tears life's special people
into pieces
by the evil of an owner...

I hope from a blink
I will find
another Friday joke
from a called father
or mother
even an uncle
but sadly
this time their laughter
was put aside.

Do I run for rescue
or should I still freeze
here by the telephone
and cry

when I don't want to leave
because I can no longer stay.

Rush takes over
when I run to see and believe;
as I enter my own store
like home
the doors close shut
behind me
but this time it no longer felt like home.

WITH A CRY

Memories of a past
feelings that have been shared
on the inside
on and on,
together.

Times we've shared together
special talks,
jokes and work,
holidays of closeness and warmth,

then the time came…
and we were forced to say
        "good-bye"
with a cry
that we will no longer stay.

We still have memories
which will always leave
us with a smile.

KEY

She stands there
has no idea
what has been torn apart…

she does not look away for one
split second
to leave us for one last joy.

Her job is to take over ours
leaving the known
unknown.

Calls out our names
as all we've worked for
counted for nothing…

when she asks for the key
I held back my tears
the only thing that gave me responsibility
now taken away.

This moment
life seemd so powerful
and in it I am weak
because around me I see
a happy family
now sad.

World oh!..world
Bike oh! Bike
what have you done
you have kept us all
frozen like stone.

SEPARATED US

Morning use to come early
to my eyes of sleep,
now the night is long
for my eyes.

Tears falling in couples
when memories haunt
all of happiness
once lived with a job
when soon the owner
separated away
like a snob.

Let's not cry,
one day we will all try
to forgive what they've done
to the love within each other
that was like stone.

THE QUITTERS

I know I am a winner
no matter what,
I know I will be needed
no matter where,
because I never quit.

I know of quitters
who lose no matter what,
I know of some sent away
no matter where
because they choose
not to win.

A winner will never quit
but a quitter will never win.

SAME

They all stand together again
myself included
each is forced to leave with one last smile,
one last joke,
one last word said of care;
taking only memories of the good
now torn apart.

Each will step into the future all over again
where things will never be the same,
Inside
I am torn apart
yet I laugh my cry
my eyes are blinded by the tears,
I know they feel the pain
but hide it for my comfort.

We stand together again
trying to face now later
rather than later now;
the only friends
now will be taken from me,
the only place
like myself
now I do not belong.

In the world such hidden treasures
now each I will
no longer see,
the many miles that I will

later run
I will never find another place the same.

STOLE
for Dad—rest in peace

Thy heart is melting for the past,
the past that keept a part of me.

From that lost part taken for granted
now I feel empty inside.

Feels like everyone has gone on
without me
and now I am lost and behind;
I will never be found.

Has the many miles come between us
or has my own heart betrayed me?

Have you ever given me a chance
to make two holes
into one whole
before my heart
you forever
stole.

BECOME OF HER

She stares at me,
tears rolling down her cheeks,
confused by the lost,
neglected by the wanted.

As I walk towards her reflection

closer to my own
softly she whispers
"what have I done?"

Her eyes wiped away from sight
where she stands no longer
with her needed part
but alone
staring through
what is left of her;
more or less nothing
since everything was taken from her
through betrayal.

Her lips speak,
sense them moving
the heart beats,
can't feel alive
her beauty remains…
can't see it anymore
unless the reflecting opposite
becomes her past.

LETTERS LIVED IN

Whispers life through the evil clouds
of living,
orders you to feel all of sorrow
to make it strive for peace,
rules against your heart
to know the unknown,
loses you bit by bit
through the echos of living end,
then death becomes you alive!

What have you now learned
or gained
other than the letters
W...O...R...L...D
that you live
through sleep
waiting to wake up.

RISE ABOVE

Blocked from the choice of living
where identity must become a hidden token,
nothing of you matters,
as long as thy words are not spoken.

Raped apart by their imaginations,
must I hear this
and keep it hurt inside?

No one matters
more than you do to yourself;
to give all of you up
for the cruelty of old age
will do no good.

Rise above the fogginess
they create,
have faith in your state
because one day when
you become them
they will be sorry
about the food they ate.

YOU ARE YOUR START

Cruelty of life sure puts you down
making you feel like everybody
wants you to drown.

Among the rich
and the poor
the healthy
and the ill,
you'll still be keept aside still.

Life sure is an amazing thrill,
striving to learn, become
and to be a part of this
that will come to an end.

Soon
what everybody makes you feel
does not count blessings
that have always been you....

Only you are your start,
if you give up now,
you might give up on the
only thing in life
that matters the most....
You!

ANOTHER CHAPTER FILLED

Echos of the past,
drips of blood to the heart;
where now only lies
of a past

can heal the emptiness felt.

There must have been something right,
something true,
that can do true justice.

You walked away
from the scene of a crime;
turned your back on all of pain
and now I am
Sailing towards the wind.

Knowing you're near
and I can not see,
I gain no happiness
nor pain
but another chapter
of an open book
filled with rain.

NEEDS ON ROAD

From a distance
mirror,
she sits waiting,
hiding from the known
betraying her heart
like an unknown.

Cement shadowed
she sees it coming,
it gets closer
sight feels no happiness
but care is here now
for itself.

His appearance
like an restless child,
does not use lips to speak
nor ears to hear
because for his heart
he does not care.

Drives around in circles
two roads reflecting
each other with needs,
from the world can not run
to be alone
for roads are passion like stone.

ESCAPE

Drives smoothly
like swimming in oil,
arms on the gear
from it thy heart he steers.

Roads are ending
places are filled
houses are owned
people are watching
the world
owns us all
where in it
escape is no goal.

NICE EYES

Bench is your couch,
your presence
like a china furniture.

Sitting softly
as I glance
The hair
strength of the army,
the eyes
beauty to love's royal
the mouth
wet by the straws.

You drink freshness
clothed as in a movie
cuffs rolled over
arms with power,
just waiting…
not knowing I'll be there.

BREAK

Blinded by the tears I've cried
missing you is just a shadow
following me
my love is a blur
I can not clear.

Existence of me is a crime
that feelings do no
true justice,
my love is a sin to your heart.

Come to my dare,
love is stronger than hate
that I can not break apart.

NOTHING CHANGED

Walked your path
spoke your tongue
cried your betrayal
       but I still...
your path I walk
your tongue I speak
your betrayal I cry.

HOLD ON TO MEMORIES

In thoughts of you,
I wrap myself tightly
bringing precious memories
into reality.
       I meet you
       I walked with you
       I laughed with you
       I cared with you
       I cry with you...today
I wanted to reach out,
to hold the inner you
but I knew if I tried
the spell would break
and you would vanish again.
So I keept my eyes closed tightly
and let your memory hold me close.

FORCED TO LEAVE

Close my eyes
turning dreams into reality
finishing off the last traces
of an unfinished painting

into a colourful world.

Sun shining
birds flying free
life such a wonderful place.

I did not want to leave
I knew if I stayed
the night would become morning
and wake me up.

So, I glanced at you
for last
and forced to say
good-bye.

EQUAL AGAIN

What would have been if…
life was too easy
love so strong
and people equally happy.

What would do harm if…
the hunger was feed
the poor made richer
and hate destroyed.

Life…
a unfair living
one road
equal
some time
along the way
separated

left uneven.

Keep faith and along the way
we will meet again.

I WALKED A LONG WAY TIL I FOUND YOU

I walked a long way…
I walked in my dreams
to meet you
but when I reached
I woke up,
I walked through glass
to find you
when I did
my feet were too sore to stay,
I walked where my heart
guided me…
I hold you now
and will never let go.

IN THOUGHT

Flipping through my address book
I reached someone
in a place with an old number,
I almost sat there frozen
in thoughts of you,
asking myself questions
of letting the past fade away
like death
becomes us.

For a moment,
I almost turned away

but in the name of truth

how do I turn
the page
the way,
I turned
my back
on someone who once
needed a friend
as much as I did,
for a single moment of
misunderstanding.

I know actions
come unwillingly sometimes,
and one's speech speaks
wrong meanings
that hurt like
a sword stabbed
right through thy heart.

But beneath all actions
and words
lies all of truth
seen only through
understanding
by a friend to a friend….

Capable of so much respect
that becomes invisible to itself.

MY FUTURE

They tell me
I am lurking in the shadows

in a future untold,
I am waiting for it to happen
but it is an mystery
that will never unfold.

They prove
I am holding impatient
blank pages of a book
that tales and stories
of mine
will not be told.

They say
I am carrying
a baggage of secrets
that will be spilled
and my future will be
determined and stilled.

Every minute
of each day and night
in my heart it seems near
enough to touch so what I hear
and see
stays completely out of sight.

Around each corner
when I turn and walk my way
they follow...
tempting, teasing me to run
but I know if I do
they will run
and I will betray myself again.

IT TAKES YOU

When you've given yourself
the chance to have a heart filled with life
you will not be another raindrop
in a sunny day.

You will not look up to the sky
and be one more cloud
that hurries and worries
frowns and complains
and lets life's precious gifts pass by.

Being happy is all up to you
misery becomes lonely
but happiness brings love.

Now be the sunshine that
makes the sky so blue
be the rainbow above that
shines laughter
because all it takes is
a heart filled with you.

DREAM ON...

Dream on...
this loss was once a seed
planted in a worm and loving garden,
days of sunshine grew this
planted seed into a bonded rose.

As it opened its soul beautifully
it started to rain
turned dried eyes wet

and washed away
a life together.

TIME HAS CHANGED US

Time goes by...
it slowly separates us,
guides us towards different directions,
it ages us
through life, dreams and memories.

Now we become another dream
time renews us,

WHOLE AGAIN

It took strength,
it took courage,
it took hope,
it took faith,
it took giving you up
til I reached myself.

I had been lost inside of you,
your heart was aching
you did not want to say it otherwise
but still you held me in you
not letting me go on.

I enjoyed staying
and enjoyed being a fool
as much as
I needed to leave
but needed some sort of tool.

I did not think strength
could be so strong,
I did not think courage
could make me see,
I did not think hope
could take me to dreams,
I did not think faith
could keep me going
until I forced myself away
and now I am whole again.

WISHING FOR A DREAM

When it is dark
I lie awake in my bed
the world seems quiet and still.

For a moment thoughts in my head
make me dream of what I wish I could have,
a cold wind blows towards my face
reminds me I am still awake.

My life is and had been
through tragedy
but still my happiness
money could not buy,
my health all of wealth could not have.

Then again...

Living happily is still hard
dreams are puzzling
through every piece set
like another shadow
just clouded another dream.

I lie awake at night
just thinking back
over and over again
until I fall asleep again
for last.

GO ON AGAIN

I must wipe my tears,
I must forget the past,
I must be strong to go on.

There is nothing of us left
there are no birds singing our song,
there are no jokes that bring us laughter
there are no feelings to bring us love,
another road has died.

New experience,
new feelings are hiding somewhere,
I may not reach right now,
it waits to bring new feelings
that reveal the past for the best,
there will be someone who will
bring laughter simply by standing there.

I must no longer
run for no future,
I must no longer
feel for a broken heart,
I must no longer
cry for this loss,
But go on again....!

I RATHER CRY NOW

I rather cry now
for the people who have turned away,
I rather be hated now
from the people who never cared.

I rather live in pain and sorrow
with a heart that is true
then happily
with a heart full of lies.

When clouds take over my sunshine
they all slowly disappear,
their backs turned away
fading before my eyes.

They saw me slowly coming towards them
meaning no harm
but they had to turn away
laughing at me
as they slowly push me away.

I rather cry now
all on my own,
when I reach happiness,
I will not look back
to listen to their cry for me
because the rain will fall
and wash me away forever.

SKY

There is a part of the sky
watching over us
Where heaven is held by the clouds.

There are the birds
flying free
whispering messages to angels.

There is a moon guiding us
through the night and day
and stars to wish upon.

Below this higher beauty
       I stand
       we stand
all alone.

Everything around us
is sleepwalking
through dream,
not looking up the sky
wishing to wake up.

OCEAN

Here by the still water,
the ocean,
a place of beauty;
to call my own.
So much like me
still of ice in the cold
and full of life through heat.
The waves swing moods

from sadness to happiness
then back again,
traveling for into the ocean
of memories and treasures
that will one day be felt.
The waves traveling free
as if nothing was blocking
its destination.
Its freedom is wide and
but limited by the ground
that ends the river and
the rocks that fight back otherwise.
The whispers from each wave,
unique and true in its own form
and voice
speaking to each other
with no greater authority
over others.
The water blue like the sky
reflecting itself through
in purity,
clothed not for fashion
but for the only blue it has.
Living only for what it is
and has,
needing no fulfillment of anything
more or less.
The ocean full of water
all of the same kind.
Unity of waves and water
pure of any sin.
Asking nothing but to fulfill
a thirst within itself.
Here by the ocean
I am alone.

One of wave and purity
traveling deep under earth
to lie my last rest through dirt.
Just wishing I was like
the water in ocean without an end.

WORLD AROUND ME

Thoughts of the world around me
slowly disappear
along with my fears,
problems and hatred;
now that I have entered a
new world.

A world different from mine,
new emotions, hopes
and dreams arise;
a sense of belonging
and understanding
replaces that of confusion.

A nation of unity,
people treated equally
a place of no social injustice,
people respected and one of acceptance.

There is no greed,
hunger, drugs or crime;
it is a world without bigotry
or ignorance.

Tears and troubles are replaced
with dreams and goals
coming alive,

it is a world of knowledge
perfection and fresh starts,
untouched by pollution
but alive with nature.

I am here now
life is a whirlwind of colours
passing by.
I come upon a river,
there I saw my reflection clear,
I thought about my life
and memories I've made
that are acknowledged in
my heart that I laid
When I decided to lay to rest.

I thought about what I'd done
then I become forced by power
to return to the world around me.

One shattered by problems
to be solved
but for those who truly made
the difference;
I left behind.
I will hurt them
just the way I am hurting.

So my sense of giving up
soon transformed into one hope.
I took a last walk around the heavens,
beside your soul
that you've given away without
a second chance.

I will now go back
hoping that one day
the distant world in my mind
will match this one
surrounding you.
But for now
I will live my time
in search of something
to hold on to,
some identity to travel
in search of a destination.

My future is waiting
somewhere in time,
I will come back to lie here
beside your grave, hurting the
ones surrounded by me now
without giving life a chance,
reason or identity.

NO ONE

You don't need anyone
to hold you,
to lie and say they care.

You don't need anyone to
answer to,
to tell all about your mistakes.

The doors to heaven do not
open to pairs that were
supporters to each other.

In heaven there are no mirrors
to reflect back,
the mistakes that you've
made.

You do not enter heaven
through a ticket of better beauty
but a ticket that is pure.

CRY FOR HELP

Hold back the tears
that pain can not wash.

When you speak,
words are bounded into knives
that no one wants to come close to.

Through the mirror of life,
rain can no longer be seen
among the clouded minds in
the blue sky.

We mistake ourselves in sight
and fly into the air of loneliness

There we cry not for the dead
but for ourselves.

We speak not that of wound
but that who only listens
when you cry for yourself.

MYSTERY WARMTH

Like a warm breeze
in a cold windy night
when you pass...
the scent of your need
and only my loneliness
draws instant attraction,
only the storm of mirrors
block.

There I stand in the cold
waiting for you to pass
for my soul to heat.
From a distance,
not far
my eyes are searching
for that instant turn of temperature.

My hands are waiting
for that touch
that I am no longer alone.

From a reflecting glass
and a board of steel
I must exit to find
what I am still searching for,
to know who keeps me
warm...
from a distance.

YOUNG GIRL

Young girl falls in love
with a man of no identity,
where she loses herself
in fear through him.
At the beach of dying love
she drowns from the tears
this ocean bears.
He watches her slowly sink
to the bottom
through his careless eyes,
he ignores the water
the sky
and the whispers above.
Young girl swims her way up
over and over again
giving fear of dying
another chance,
each time digs herself further
through the soil of the living dead.
Young girl is alone
and heartbroken,
mistaken and mislead
by the evil side of man
that when the sweet melody
she hears
Young girl goes back
to meet her love at the beach
to give drowning another chance.
Young girl—the man is behind you.

WIND

When across an open door
you see what you may not have,
it comes to you,
slowly it opens your eyes,
your ears listen to the
slow motion of the wind.
Its surrender leaves smiles
on your tender lips
then slowly reaches for your heart.
There the numbness starts from your head to toe
bringing an intense beauty
from the inside out then it leaves...
There are no maps to trace
the wind
there are no tracks to follow
it has left all at once
promising no way back.
The wind travels
to unknown skies
forbidden to be felt.

FRIEND

The moment life gets dull,
I look away
across an open store
like wishing upon a star,
this time it is not dark,
where my tears
star don't see
this time it is not a
one way street.
I use to speak

no star heard.
This time it is not a dream
or an imagination
that I glance at every night,
I am not speaking to the clouds
of never ending rain
But a friend,
The more I unwrap
the personality,
one of caring and kind,
the more I tremble through
my own fear of what happiness is
Friend brings back that lost smile,
that dry tear
and the beauty my mirror stole.
Friend takes over the million stars
and becomes one that
brings me back to who I really am.

WHAT IS HATE?

THE NAME, THE FACE, THE KISS,
ALL THAT ONCE WAS TRUE
NOW HE HAS SOMEONE NEW.

THE LOVE THAT WE ONCE SHARED
IT WAS ALL AN ACT THAT HE ONCE CARED
ALL THE TIME WE SPENT TOGETHER
NOW HE IS GONE FOREVER.

THE FAVORITE SONG WE PLAYED TOGETHER
THE SORROW, THE LONG NIGHT
HOW LOST HE MADE ME FEEL
NOW OUR LOVE IS GOING NOWHERE.

THE MEMORY OF HIS CERTAIN WALK
THE EMPTY WORDS HE USE TO TALK
ALL THE THINGS HE USE TO SAY
HE PROMISED HE WILL NEVER BETRAY
BUT NOW HE IS GONE AWAY.

THAT LOVING GENTLE WAY
WHEN I MEET HIM ON THAT DAY
THE STUPID THINGS HE MADE ME DO
AND NOW HE LOVES HER TOO.

THE WAY HE TRILLED WHEN I WALKED BY
NOW ALL BRINGS ME TO CRY
THE LOVING WAY HE SPOKE MY NAME
AND NOW THINGS ARE NOT THE SAME.

ALL OF THE TIME THAT WENT TOO FAST
THEY ARE ALL GONE AND IN THE PAST
HE PROMISED HIS LOVE WILL LEAVE ME NEVER
BUT NOW HE IS GONE FOREVER.

NEEDING TO FORGET FROM HELP
SENT FROM ABOVE
NOW AFTER ALL THIS TIME,
HE GOES ON WITH LIFE,
HE DOES NOT WAIT
THAT IS WHEN I REALIZE
THAT THIS LOVE WAS HATE!

ANOTHER TEAR

Shed not another tear my dear eyes
fight back another sword
against thy heart.

Speak not another word of sadness
sing the song of happiness
that all sorrow will bring.

Miss not the unexisting heart,
wasting another minute
is not worthwhile.

Pick up the memories
hold on to
own feelings,
trash away all betrayal
just take all of real.

Cover up all of sensitivity
become strength
unlock the heart of steel
bring about the inner you
that is really real
because the soul will not
bear another tear.

STORE CORNER

The fragrance of old dreams
I pass by fairly
the light that welcomed me in
no longer exists.

As I pass
a cold wind blows towards my soul
making memories so cold.

As I glance in
tears well up in my eyes
hoping a past becomes my dream
when from my mistakes
now my heart learned how to scream.

A place...
I can describe it as is
I can sense all actions happen
I can feel how it all started
but I can not make up
the meaning of it all.

As I pass
I do not miss the heart that
words only spoke truth
I miss what lightened the store corner
when I passed by ......

FEEL AND TELL

Ask the heart
do not trust the thought
because only the heart
can feel and tell.

STRONGER

Why do we bring more rain
when it is already raining
Why do we step on roses
when it lives no longer
Why do we become weak
when our love is much stronger.

EVERYTHING REVEALED

My mouth has spoken
the words that needed to be said,
my heart has felt
the feelings that needed to be revealed,
my feet have run
the many miles that needed to be run.
I reach a place,
so strange where my dreams are turned upside down,
minute by minute,
living wasted by worry and
love that gains no life.

soon, I realized that dreams take time
to come true,
as hopes work the mind closer to dreams,
life is lived once
why let nothing come on the way
of a life given only to you.

WAR

Like a soldier,
lost between empty words,
haunted by a past,
missing every trace
that never said its last.
Through the clouds that come and go,
I watch our love slowly burning low.
Frightened by the falling rain,
hoping for a part of you to remain.
Washed away among tears
our last touch become this present fear.
Promises still remain unfolded
through the breeze of a past,
forgotten deep below the war between
your other.

COME TRUE

Speak the words of truth
you may never fear
Promise what will be done
you may never gear
Walk the direction you want
you may never lose track
Show the feelings you feel
you may never be mistaken
Reach for what is near
you may never fall
Dream a little bit longer
and everything will come true.

LOSS

Speaks softly
trembles with words
hurt by echoes from my heart

comes towards me
the eyes of beauty tear
the smile full of fear

reaches for a hand but scared to touch
wants to say the things that show care
but what I said, now he is scared to dare.

Within him I see pain,
now feels what I felt
learns a mistake
the way he mistook

Admits a loss
that he has made
when a chance with no chance
he turned away from
and looked into a different direction

Left me frozen
given me no direction,
now I must leave
to correct my destination.

HOW

How could words mean nothing
how could promises never come true
how did we lose all we dreamt of
how did we drift apart when nature
gave us a chance.
Why do we both need to suffer
when all we want we may just reach for.

WHAT AM I SUPPOSED TO SAY?
for Dad—rest in peace

Brought me into this world,
as you take your leave,
what am I supposed to say?
"..thank you for not standing by my side..."
or must I just imagine you did love me
when you choose death over me!

What is the heart when it does not beat
what is the picture when it does not speak
how do I know your life was so weak?

In me lies emotions searching for someone,
someone who could have made my dreams
come alive,
my living a little bit easier
and wipe my tears a little bit more.

You betrayed all that I needed
you left me when you were most missed,
how could you turn your back on me
the way you did when I know
my innocence took your life.

LEARN AS YOU GO

It is not a choice
to live or die
but it is a choice
to live right or wrong.

Life offers you all,
from it you must decide
your own destination
to mistake without knowledge
is not a wrong
but to take advantage of a mistake
is a crime.

There are no more people here for you
than you might think,
you would not have showed up
if you did not belong,
you were brought by a timeless love
and nothing is more welcoming.

Life offers different levels
called steps of wisdom
to experience it all
you will enter heaven to be given
your reward.

So never doubt yourself wrong
give yourself credit,
that people can honour
to accomplish you.

To fail is you
and it is your reward of learning
so live your time

and learn as you go.

YOUR TIME

Dreams are needs
hopes full of faith
times full of waiting
until everybody is sitting
and you are standing.

ME AND THE WORLD

I was no longer alone in this world
thought I become a part of it
belonged for my own success
but the success in me counts for nothing.

Softness of my skin
roughened by thought
the veins of life taken away
turning the sweetness of my blood
so sour and cold
tearing the love within a broken heart apart

Understood in lies
when spoken the words of truth,
my own soul taken away
against myself
the life in me no longer lives
every hour another scars this heart
using knives.

Where have I come
why am I here
because this world no one can bare.

How do I know when to stay or go
when do I know it is my turn to row
because til now I am tied like a bow
and all of days the hour slow.

HAPPY

The sunshine lightens the heart
that special call
that only words speak forgiveness.

No more tears
happiness has spoken
care has been shown
but lies never forgotten.

Tell me how do I ever learn
to trust thy heart again,
when all this time
fell in care of your lies
when you made me believe,
when your heart I wanted to strive.

Let me go on again
this one more time
happy, less than joy
hurt but more than pain
together but still alone
because everything is gone
I am happy!

FLYING

Like two birds
in the sky we crossed paths

that gave us both one breath
to complete two breathings
longing for a friend.

We sat·on the tree top,
enjoyed living on the top of the world,
the sun was shining bright...

when the rain came
we both got torn apart
by the clouds that took over us.

I fled high and low
to find you
through mountains and seas
to reach you
but soon I was out of breath
so I gave up.

I felt dropped down
when in my sleep you turned away,
where I landed
I rested my head
and slowly closed my eyes
as if I was going back to sleep once again.

YOU ARE YOUR START

Cruelty of life sure puts you down
making you feel like everybody
wants you to drown.

Among the rich
and the poor
the healthy

and the ill,
you'll still be kept aside still.

Life sure is an amazing thrill,
striving to learn, become
and to be a part of this
that will come to an end.

Soon
what everybody makes you feel
does not count blessings
that have always been you....

Only you are your start,
if you give up now,
you might give up on the
only thing in life
that matters the most—
You!

SHE

Another year has gone,
another tear wiped away,
another chapter of an open book
days torn in pieces since the last look.

Through a reflecting glass
I become her,
deep brown eyes like stone
with a smile of innocence
still dreaming
when sleep has awaken all night.

The words she speaks,

the lips do not move,
the music she hears
is what the heart never bears.

She looks at me as we were one,
I must help
but something blocks us part
when I move
the closer I go
the move of my own reflection
darkens our distance.

She becomes flat
very like myself,
through a square cut photo
cries when I cry
leaves when I leave
because she is my reflection through the mirror

SENSITIVE FIGURE

The heart,
sensitive figure
made of two curving lines
let not its shine be taken by a scratch
let not lies destroy its beauty
let not the tears melt down its colour
let not the world take its strength
but most important
let not love break it in half
when truth is whole.

THIS IS IT

Through good times and bad
you have fallen,
you have given all of you
to gain only more rain,
this is what we call
experiencing pain.

Through laughter and crying
you have been neglected,
you have tried to fit with the crowd
but found yourself alone,
this is what we call
experiencing loneliness.

Through the old and the new
you have lived it
and are still living it,
you have come so far
now you have reached heaven
this is what we call
The Journey Of A Fragile Heart.